The Vitra Design Museum
Frank Gehry Architect

The Vitra Design Museum
Frank Gehry Architect

Text by Olivier Boissière
and Martin Filler
Photographs by Richard Bryant

RIZZOLI
NEW YORK

First published in the United States of America in 1990 by
RIZZOLI INTERNATIONAL PUBLICATIONS, INC.
300 Park Avenue South, New York, NY 10010

Copyright © 1990 Verlag Gerd Hatje, Stuttgart, 1990
Photographs © Richard Bryant, 1990

ISBN 0-8478-1199-9
LC 89-63961

English language translation by Michael Robinson

Printed and bound in West Germany

Contents

Foreword   6
Alexander von Vegesack

Vitra Design Museum, Weil am Rhein   8
Frank Gehry

Veni, Vidi, Vitra: 10
The International Architecture
of Frank Gehry
Martin Filler

Manufacturing the Sublime   24
Olivier Boissière

Construction of Vitra Design Museum   36
and Furniture Production Unit

Foreword

Alexander von Vegesack

The idea of the Vitra Design Museum grew out of a furniture producer's wish to find and document the roots and history of his craft. Rolf Fehlbaum, director of the Vitra furniture business, embarked upon his search in the early eighties.

Trying to find his own roots very quickly led to discoveries which broke the confines of the original plan. Intensive concern with the history of industrially produced furniture opened the collector's eyes to the enormous variety of the subject.

The collector's passion was linked to the insight that examining the past could give new impetus to the furniture of tomorrow.

Rolf Fehlbaum and I met in 1986. He told me about his intention of commissioning a building to house his growing collection. The architect of his choice was the American Frank O. Gehry. Gehry and Fehlbaum had met in 1984, when Claes Oldenburg and Coosje van Bruggen were installing their sculpture, "Balancing Tools", on the Vitra site. The first plan was for a new production unit with an adjacent "home" for the collection. But a mutually stimulating discussion developed between architect and client, in which what was originally peripheral became a central theme. This was the point at which I became involved in the project.

I was immediately enthusiastic about the idea of a new museum. We soon moved away from the original idea of a closed private collection. A plan emerged for a museum accessible to the general public, and the Vitra Design Museum first opened its doors in November 1989. The collection was systematically extended while the museum was being built. Until then it had largely grown according to the subjective taste of its founder. Now it includes almost all important periods and styles of international furniture design. It ranges from the beginning of industrial mass production in the mid nineteenth century via the Arts and Crafts movement, to later designs by Viennese architects and the Rietveld experiments and Bauhaus period functionalism, down to international post-war developments, ending for the time being with eighties avant-garde furniture sculptures. Charles Eames' work forms the centerpiece of the collection: his brilliant construction concepts were a basis for a new design aesthetic after the Second World War.

In contrast to other museums, in which furniture design is only one subject among many, the Vitra Design Museum focuses principally upon its historical and future development. Public interest in this sphere of everyday culture has continued to increase in the last few years. But while design has become a fashionable notion, now used to cover "styling" of any kind, knowledge about its theory and practice is restricted to a small and élite circle of experts. Our main aim for the museum is to make it an "antiélite" institution which appeals to the layman and awakes his awareness of a designed environment.

Vitra Design Museum exhibitions concentrate on presenting objects occupying key positions in the development of industrial furniture design because of their material, construction, function, and form. The aim is to increase knowledge of furniture and convey criteria for choosing it. Both historical developments and present-day tendencies are analysed from constantly changing points of view. Part of the aim is to make the whole process of an emerging design, from idea to completed end product, perfectly clear and comprehensible in its logic at all stages of its development.

Faithful reproductions of originals are intended to shake the visitor out of his passive attitude and invite him to active experience. In this museum we say: "Please do touch!" Direct bodily contact can easily convey new experiences, and make it possible to grasp design. Design quality is not understood merely in the head; it should also be experienced by the body.

Although furniture forms the core of the collection, we also intend the museum's activities to turn to subjects beyond the interior, like space and architecture. Frank O. Gehry's museum design not only invites us to do that – it imposes a welcome obligation.

Vitra Design Museum, Weil am Rhein

Frank Gehry

I traveled to Weil am Rhein the first time with my family and the Oldenburgs, Claes and his wife/collaborator Coosje van Bruggen. They were there to inspect the final touches on their sculpture and then set its final location in front of the Vitra Furniture complex. I can't remember why I was there.

Vitra is owned by the Fehlbaum family, and the sons, represented by brother Rolf Fehlbaum, commissioned the sculpture to celebrate their father's 70th birthday. Given my experience with siting buildings and my chance presence at the site, and given too that I will not shrink from offering advice when asked – I was, and did.

I met Rolf Fehlbaum a year or two earlier at the Oldenburg's loft in New York and was informed that he was the person who had written to me several times (in the year or two before we met) to explore the possibility of designing a chair for Vitra. The requests were languishing in a hold basket only because I had just been through the exhilarating but equally debilitating experience of creating a line of paper furniture called Easy Edges. I was determined not to be distracted from architecture again. I was caught in my negligence to answer his kind letters and agreed (since he was a nice, friendly, knowledgeable guy) to pursue the design of a chair for Vitra sometime in the future. Several chairs and meetings later, Rolf asked me to design a small furniture study museum and a factory for Vitra near the Tool Gate sculpture.

The brief was modest, the collection was modest, and the expectations were modest; reflective of the character of the Fehlbaum family. Since it was to be my debut in Europe, Rolf kindly gave me the leeway, time and encouragement to make it a good one.

My intention was to understand and extrapolate from the context. I wanted the new buildings to set up a dialogue with the wonderful existing plant designs by Grimshaw. The relationship to the highway, the green hills across the road, the smaller scale buildings of the adjacent town including the car dealership on the adjacent site and of course the sculpture all became issues.

My solution is an urban village which places the study museum in the front. Perhaps it's a sculptor's strategy – but by coopting the language of the building for the two flanking entrances to the simple factory buildings behind, compositionally includes the factory building in the perception of the museum and vice versa.

The simple white factory building with large industrial windows is both contrasting and respectful of the existing high tech expression of the original factory. Yet to me it seems as if the new building was built before the "sleek Metroliner" retaining the original building's modern preeminence. This notion tickles me since I took my building's cues from the Grimshaw project. Mr. Grimshaw expressed the stairs, toilets and storage components of his building as towers like servo mechanisms outside but attached to the simple factory office box. I used this same idea in both the new factory and study museum with a slightly different "twist." So the original sleek modern has spawned a neighbor that speaks to its origins, allows it to remain the Godfather of Modernism and yet appears otherworldly.

The complexity of the exterior happily does not interfere with the background role that is necessary for a room in which to view sculptural objects. The gallery space was kept intentionally basic with natural top light.

Now the problem is success. The Fehlbaums have acquired an extraordinary collection five times the size of the original program. They have a director of international stature; the potential is evident. The just completed building needs some minor adjustments, to say the least.

A key participator in the Vitra endeavor, to whom I extend my deepest thanks, is "mein lieber Herr Pfeifer" – Günter Pfeifer, and his partner Roland Mayer, who gave me professional assistance, advice and staff in collaboration as executive architect, producing and supervising the documents and construction. I am most appreciative.

From my office, I expected and received extraordinary effort, led by my partner Robert Hale with major help from Berthold Penkhues, a young architect from Germany who was doing time in our office. The others on my staff to mention and thank for their assistance are: Greg Walsh, Edwin Chan and C. S. Bonura.

Veni, Vidi, Vitra:
The International Architecture of Frank Gehry

Martin Filler

Among artists of the highest order there is a very wide range of development – or a lack thereof – over the course of a career. There are some artists who briefly achieve greatness early in their lives but never again rise to that level of inspiration. Then there are those who attain a certain high plateau of creativity but remain there, neither declining nor significantly growing. And finally there is the smallest group of all – those artists who continue to deepen and expand with age, leaving behind impressive earlier efforts while moving ever forward into new realms of expression. At the age of 60, Frank Gehry can claim a rightful place in that final category. Ample confirmation of that is given by his Vitra Design Museum of 1986–89 in Weil am Rhein, West Germany. This structure is that rarest of all architectural phenomena: a building that is at once a landmark as well as a breakthrough. It stands out in an œuvre already filled with advances in the art of architecture, but it also points to new directions for Gehry, with its intimations of his growing mastery of interior space that might in due course place him among the greatest architects of this waning century.

Gehry's formal inventions have already set him apart from most of his contemporaries during a period of extraordinary plagiarism in architecture, which has always been an art of emulation but has become even more overtly so at a time when direct appropriation is a legitimate artistic premise. Although the extreme stylistic excesses of some Late Modernist "form givers" led to a reactionary desire for a return to order and tradition – culminating in the Postmodern Classicism of the seventies and eighties – a few members of the international avant-garde have steadfastly refused to embrace an approach they deem essentially derivative and retrograde. In the United States there have been no more convincing exponents of that independent position, neither Modernist nor Postmodernist, than Peter Eisenman und Frank Gehry, the former with a strong interest in linguistic theory, the latter with a strong interest in contemporary art.

Unquestionably the role of art in architecture – or the acknowledgement of architecture as an art form – has been one of the major preoccupations of the eighties, but characteristically Gehry has addressed the question quite differently than his Postmodernist colleagues. They have proposed a revival of applied ornament, the reintroduction of programmatic iconography, and the integration of painting, sculpture, and applied crafts into architecture much in the same way it was done before the rise of the International Style. Symptoms of the results such an outlook is likely to stimulate could be found in the generally feeble schemes generated by the exhibition "Collaboration: Artists & Architects," sponsored by the Architectural League of New York in observance of its centennial and shown in that city in 1981–82. The eleven invited architects each selected artists with whom to work in concert on a project that would suggest a new synthesis of mediums. Regrettably, few of the proposals reached the level of competence, let alone the excellence that had been hoped for. Most of the architects succeeded in limiting the artists' participation to the decoration of their buildings, the usual subservient role to which art has been relegated under such superficially "collaborative" circumstances. Almost alone among the "Collaboration" show's submissions demonstrating the truly invigorating possibilities of an authentic exchange between an artist and an architect was the entry of Gehry and Richard Serra. Their proposal for a fantastic tubular cable bridge connecting New York's Chrysler Building with an enormous sculpture of a fish jutting out of New York harbor was a rare instance of an almost complete blurring of artistic categories – the art was architecture and the architecture was art.

It is that conception of a building – not as a surface for a container of art, but rather as a work of art in and of itself – that gives Gehry's buildings, especially those for cultural institutions, a significance well beyond those of most other architects working today.

One of the ironies of Gehry's otherwise extraordinarily successful career has been that thus far this supreme exponent of architecture as art has had few chances to design art museums. He has demonstrated unusual versatility and sympathy as the designer of temporary exhibitions at the Los Angeles County Museum of Art, including the shows "Art Treasures of Japan" (1965), "Billy Al Bengston" (1968), "The Avant-Garde in Russia 1910–1930" (1980), "Seventeen Artists in the Sixties" (1981), and "German Expressionist Sculpture" (1983). His surprising, energetic schemes for non-art museums – his Cabrillo Marine Museum of 1979 in San Pedro, Califor-

Frank Gehry and Richard Serra. Project for a bridge at New York. Above, Chrysler Building with the tubular bridge connection; below, sketch of the bridge. Exhibition "Collaboration: Artists & Architects," Architectural League, New York, 1981–82.

Cabrillo Marine Museum, San Pedro, California, 1979.

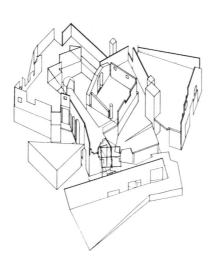

Children's Museum, Los Angeles, California, 1980. Axonometric.

nia, Children's Museum of 1980 in Los Angeles, and California Aerospace Museum of 1982–84 in Los Angeles – have likewise proven his ability to deal with both limited budgets and widely differing programmatic needs. His personal activities as an art collector and friend of virtually every important figure on the contemporary Los Angeles art scene, and a number of international stature as well, have given additional evidence of his superb qualifications for art-museum commissions, and yet they have continued to elude him.

This happened most surprisingly in his home city of Los Angeles. Gehry was passed over for the design of the coveted Museum of Contemporary Art in favor of the Japanese architect Arata Isozaki. With what can only be termed reverse chauvinism, the museum's officials sought to avoid being characterized as a regional, rather than international, institution, and thus selected a foreign architect instead of the world-acclaimed and accomplished local master. Partly in response to the negative reaction caused by this slight to Gehry – more stinging because it came from just those international architectural circles MOCA sought to impress – Gehry was subsequently asked by MOCA to design its Temporary Contemporary Gallery, an interim display space not far from the construction site for the new structure and meant to be used until the Isozaki building was completed. If anything, Gehry's brilliant 1983 conversion of an old police garage into the Temporary Contemporary was greeted with far more critical approval than Isozaki's somewhat disappointing MOCA, and the putatively makeshift TC (as it is now called in LA) has been retained as a permanent part of the institution in response to its status as one of the most admired new museums created in America during a decade of intense activity in that building type. Indeed, the particular success of the Temporary Contemporary has caused a problem for Gehry, who has had several potential clients approach him for similar conversion of abandoned industrial or commercial structures for use as art galleries. Though he did make one such remodeling after MOCA – his Edgemar Museum of 1987–89 in Santa Monica, California, a former dairy plant now the anchor of a multi-use commercial complex – he has had to decline others, pointing out to would-be patrons that the ability to replicate the effect of the Temporary Contemporary is wholly dependent on the quality of the building proposed for renovation; some are suitable, others not.

Museums of architecture and design raise certain issues that do not necessarily have a bearing on institutions devoted to painting and sculpture. Perhaps because of the pioneering Department of Architecture and Design established at the Museum of Modern Art in New York in 1930, the connection of those two disciplines in a museum have been taken for granted in a way that the affinities between art and architecture have not. In fact, during the museum building boom of the 1980s, one pronounced tendency was a preference for a neutral, self-effacing architecture deemed by many to be less competitive with the art on display than designs of a more assertive architectonic character. It is interesting to note, however, that a boldly expressed architectural presence need not detract from the clear and sympathetic display of works of art or design. One of the most critically well-received buildings of the past decade was James Stirling's and Michael Wilford's Neue Staatsgalerie of 1977–84 in Stuttgart. Though its exterior could scarcely be more architecturally attention-getting – abounding in dozens of the visual jests and historical plays so typical of Stirling's oeuvre – the exhibition galleries themselves are coolly neutral, providing flexible, unobtrusive spaces for showing art of every period to potentially maximum advantage.

Oddly, the two major design museums built in Germany during the eighties are considerably less effective in balancing architectural design with the practical requirements of display. O. M. Ungers' German Architecture Museum of 1979–84 in Frankfurt and its close neighbor, Richard Meier's Museum for the Decorative Arts, also of 1979–84, are neither the most inspired examples of their architects' abilities nor have they proven to be particularly hospitable to the kinds of objects that will most often be displayed within them. The gleaming late modernist aura of the Meier building, highly transparent and dazzlingly reflective, makes the pre-modern decorative objects and furniture of the Decorative Arts museum look lifeless and dingy, not surprising in that they were created for interiors composed of very different materials, colors, and light conditions. And the ungenerous, boxy pro-

Temporary Contemporary Gallery, Los Angeles, California, 1983.

Edgemar Museum, Santa Monica, California, 1987–89.

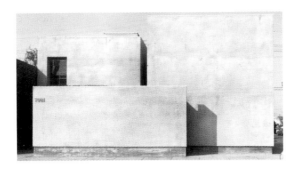

Studio-Residence for Lou Danziger,
Hollywood, California, 1964.
Entrance side at Melrose Avenue.

Rouse Company Headquarters, Columbia,
Maryland, 1974.

14

portions of the galleries in the Ungers building – certainly restricted by the dimensions of the existing villa within which the architect had to work his remodeling – are likewise not conducive to creating an atmosphere in which ideas about architectural space and volume can be effectively conveyed.

Thus Frank Gehry's Vitra Design Museum can instantly be placed in the forefront of the new German museum of the eighties not least of all because of the way in which it creates an architectural setting that is at once receptive to the display requirements of its permanent collection (furniture, and particularly chairs, of the modernist age beginning with the early experiments of Michael Thonet in the 1830s) as well as suggestive of the highest powers of architecture as an art form. The way in which Gehry manages to balance the purely practical programmatic requirements of a building with the discretionary choices that raise construction to the level of architecture has always been one of his particular strengths, and has its roots in his long years as a real-estate developer's architect before he emerged on the avant-garde scene fairly late in his career.

Gehry, following his graduation from the University of Southern California School of Architecture in Los Angeles in 1954, embarked on almost a decade of work for various large-scale architectural firms before setting up his own practice in 1962. Although Gehry soon produced what is considered by most critics to be his first high-style architectural design – the Louis Danziger studio-residence of 1964 in Hollywood, California – he continued, for another decade beyond that, to devise efficient, budget-conscious schemes for commercial clients with much less interest in aesthetic concerns than in economical solutions to very specific programmatic requirements. Following his last major work for his most important client during his first phase of independent practice, the headquarters of the Rouse Company in Columbia, Maryland, in 1974, Gehry decided, at the age of 45, to concentrate on those commissions most likely to yield the artistic component he felt had been lacking in his work up to that point. That new outlook was stimulated by his increasing contact with the young avant-garde artists – including John Altoon, Chuck Arnoldi, Larry Bell, Billy Al Bengston, Tony Berlant, Ron Davis,

Laddie John Dill, Ed Moses, Ken Price, and Ed Ruscha – who were beginning to establish Los Angeles for the first time in its history as a center of innovative visual arts (with the obvious exception of motion pictures, which have been the focus of that city's creative life for almost eighty years). Typically, Gehry's involvement with those artists was not theoretical or philosophical, but instead concerned the actual making of art and its physical processes. Gehry has frequently described himself as a "hands-on" architect – one very immediately engaged in not just the act of building, but also in the manipulation of forms as a primary design method. This runs directly counter to the increasing importance of drawing in American architecture during Gehry's past fifteen years of artistic ascendance. While most of his avant-garde colleagues have relied more and more on the drawing as their primary conceptual aid (often to less than satisfactory ends, such as in the work of Michael Graves, who has built far less convincingly than he draws), Gehry's use of models as the basis for working out his schemes, and not just representing them after the fact of design, stems straight from his observation of the working methods of the emergent Los Angeles School of the late sixties and early seventies.

Gehry's architectural training has also been a valuable source of instruction for those same painters. For example, Gehry recalls giving Ron Davis lessons in point perspective at a time when the dimensional representation of geometric forms in space began to interest the painter in his own work. The house and studio that Gehry designed for Davis in 1972 at Malibu, California, is correctly seen as a collaborative extension of their joint investigations, playing as it does with conflicting notions of actual and perceived perspective. As Rosemarie Haag Bletter has observed, it was in the Davis project that "Gehry initiated his own startling commentary on the convoluted relationship between art and architecture. A trapezoidal plan and elevations create a subtly enigmatic form, referring to but also exaggerating our normal perspectival perception of orthogonal architecture... But toying with a conflation of the world of perception and conception provides a fascinating game for Gehry's tricky sensibility. In the Ron Davis studio any automatic deduction from perceived to built reality is confounded by his construction

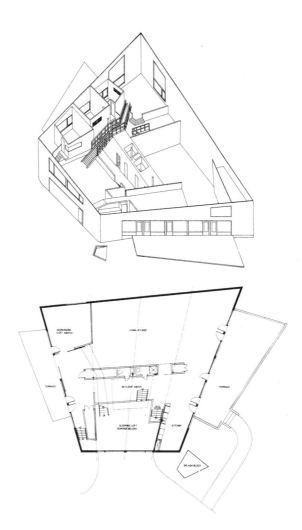

Ron Davis House, Malibu, California, 1972. Axonometric and plan.

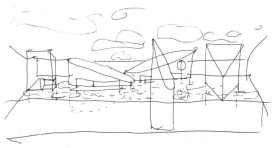

Jung Institute, Los Angeles, California, 1976. Conceptual sketch.

Wosk Residence, Beverly Hills, California, 1982–84. Sketch.

16

of what is usually only a perceptual reality, i.e., trapezoidal forms. It is as if a Renaissance architect had tried to use perspective in the execution, not just the rendering, of a building."

The most important next step in Gehry's pursuit of radical new forms of architectural design informed by art came in his unexecuted 1976 scheme for the Jung Institute in Los Angeles. Gehry's well-known conceptual sketch, though highly schematic, nonetheless reads very clearly as the primary antecedent of Gehry's works of the eighties which utilize a sculptural assemblage of strong, abstract forms: his Wosk residence of 1982–84 in Beverly Hills, California; California Aerospace Museum of 1982–84 in Los Angeles; Winton guest house of 1983–84 in Minneapolis, Minnesota; and culminating in the Vitra Design Museum. In each instance, the precise arrangement of architectural volumes was established by an intriguing balance of pragmatic concerns – such as the logical sequence of living spaces in the residences and the exhibition requirements of the museums – with an arbitrary aesthetic sense of how the forms would work together in a purely compositional sense.

Despite the cumulative liveliness of all those schemes which led up to Vitra, none of them went as far as the new design museum does in taking Gehry's formal juxtapositions to their logical – or illogical – climax: the interpenetration of those previously discrete forms to create internal volumes of an originality and surprise equal to those of the exterior. Gehry's innate sculptural skill (which accounts for his successful partnerships with Richard Serra and Claes Oldenburg, the latter being his most frequent artist-collaborator in recent years) has made it possible for him to create interior spaces that, for all their irregularity, possess a proportional and scalar appropriateness that one would be tempted to call Classical were it not for the deeply anti-Classical nature of almost all that Gehry has designed (with a few notable exceptions such as his Loyola Law School of 1981–84 in Los Angeles). Ironically, it is the Post-Modern Classicists who have had a much more difficult time of making architecture that feels as convincing in three dimensions as it appears in the two dimensions of the drawing. Again, it is obviously Gehry's determination to think of his work as objects in – or objects creating – space that accounts for this important difference between his architecture and that of some of his best-known contemporaries.

Once Gehry began to emerge during the late seventies as one of America's most interesting architectural innovators, there were those critics who were quick to warn that his particular improvisational strengths would not translate very well to other parts of the world, so specific to the Southern California climate and cultural context were his materials and construction methods. Gehry has often been quoted as saying that he does not hold any building materials to be inherently disreputable, despite the humble connotations that many Americans feel pertain to chain link fencing, unfinished plywood, corrugated metal, and wire-mesh glass, to mention only four of the favorites in his astonishingly wide palette of building products. His rumored inability to deal with anything more costly or substantial was laid to rest by the antithetically luxurious materials he employed in the Wosk apartment – including marble, granite, and lacquer – in close proximity and piquant contrast to several of his old favorites. But as Gehry himself has pointed out, "I like the juxtaposition of cheaper materials against the richer ones. It's certainly an old idea. Louis Kahn did that years ago."

Of special relevance in Gehry's expansion of his range of materials is his Winton guest house. In the harsh northern climate of Minnesota, where Gehry had to be much more concerned with the durability and weathering properties of materials than in the gentle climate of Southern California, he was able to achieve some of the very same effects of his earlier work with very little loss of the immediacy that has been a hallmark of style. For example, one prow-like bedroom wing of the Winton guest house of 1983–84 is clad in Kasota stone, a limestone native to the Minnesota region. Yet from even a short distance away it more closely resembles the unfinished plywood Gehry would have used in Los Angeles than it does travertine, which Kasota stone can look like if it is dressed and detailed more selfconsciously than is Gehry's wont.

Similarly, it was also believed that so many of Gehry's formal references were made in relation to the Southern California vernacular that his architecture would not travel convincingly to other regional contexts. It is true that Gehry has

California Aerospace Museum, Los Angeles, California, 1982–84.

Loyola Law School, Los Angeles, California, 1981–84.

Winton Guest House, Wayzata near Minneapolis, Minnesota, 1983–84.

Rudolf Steiner. Second Goetheanum,
Dornach, Switzerland, 1924–28.

Le Corbusier. Chapel of Notre-Dame du
Haut, Ronchamp, France, 1951–55.

consciously limited his detailing to a fairly mini-
mal level of finish in keeping with the relatively
low capabilities of the construction trades in the
Los Angeles region today. But he has shown
himself able to stimulate craftsmen to excep-
tional results in other contexts, such as the
superb metalwork that he supervised for the in-
stallation of his traveling exhibition "The Architecture of Frank Gehry," which opened at the
Walker Art Center in Minneapolis in 1986. In
fact, it has been Gehry's experience that the
more idiosyncratic one of his designs is, the
more likely it is to capture the imagination of
workmen who rise to the occasion with greater
alacrity than when confronted with easier but
more routine designs. That certainly was the
case with the Vitra Design Museum, which
succeeds in no small measure because of its
meticulous execution.

Vitra is a departure for Gehry in several important ways. Although he is prone to respond to
larger notions of context than most of his critics
have recognized (Gehry himself has often been a
source of that misunderstanding, preferring to
give somewhat disingenuous accounts of his design method as thoroughly *ad hoc*, with little of
the deliberate influences that most of his co-pro-
fessionals are only too happy to divulge), Vitra is
noteworthy for his open admission that two
early-twentieth century landmarks not far from
Weil am Rhein figured importantly in his conception: Rudolf Steiner's second Goetheanum of
1924–28 at Dornach, Switzerland, and Le
Corbusier's Chapel of Notre-Dame du Haut of
1951–55 at Ronchamp, France. At the opening
ceremonies for the Vitra Design Museum, Gehry
spoke eloquently of those two highly individua-
listic monuments having had a formative effect
on his newest design, which is indeed of a piece
with the idiosyncratic nature of those two earlier
pilgrimage points in that corner of Europe.

The highly expressive, and even Expressionist,
nature of the Vitra Design Museum is certainly
similar in some respects to both Steiner's and Le
Corbusier's schemes. The exterior of Vitra,
though not as seemingly hand-molded as either
the Goetheanum or the Ronchamp chapel, does
share with them a kind of crystalline massing, a
dynamic juxtaposition of orthogonal and dia-
gonal line, of massive and precarious form, that
gives them all a simultaneous feeling of stasis
and movement, resolution and tension, that is

rarely found in architecture. Given Gehry's constant efforts to infuse architecture with qualities not commonly associated with it – in fact envying the spontaneity that painters and sculptors can give their artifacts, which architects so rarely are able to equal, or even approximate – it is not surprising that these two offbeat works settled in his imagination.

Though it is by no means its most salient feature to most viewers, Vitra is also a departure for Gehry in that it is his first all-white building. His use of color in the past, although not as literal in its intentions as Michael Graves's attempts to re-establish a representational palette in architecture, has nonetheless been more wide-ranging than was the case either with the late modernists or his generational contemporaries among the "Whites" of New York or the "Silvers" of Southern California. But the much more visually unsettled massing of the Vitra Museum seemed to Gehry to need the unifying monochromatic coherence of white, and there is no question that Gehry's sculptural intentions would not be as strikingly legible had he articulated portions of the structure in different colors. Furthermore, as it stands out against the vineyard-covered landscape of its rural setting, the Vitra Museum also brings to mind the small but intense explosions of architectural form that dot the German country landscape in the form of Baroque churches, frequently no less startling in their unexpected locales than the Vitra Museum is in its. The ecclesiastical analogy might be extended further by citing the cruciform central tower of the museum, with its cross-shaped skylight surmounting the central exhibition gallery below it. It is, however, a shape clearly discernible only when one looks at a plan of the structure, which explains much but reveals little as to how Gehry has created such remarkable effects of space and light within such a small building of only 800 square meters. It is with respect to Gehry's brilliant, almost mystical, use of natural light that Vitra most readily invites comparison to Ronchamp. If Vitra does not have the richly plastic wall fabric of Notre-Dame du Haut, with its feeling of dense masonry punctuated by tunnel-like shafts of light, Gehry's sophisticated disguise of natural light through indirect sources does modulate space in an equally mysterious and absorbing manner. In fact, Gehry creates the aura of a sacred space far more convincingly

Le Corbusier. Chapel of Notre-Dame du Haut, Ronchamp, France, 1951–55. Interior view.

than most church architects have done in the 35 years since Ronchamp, and if art has indeed become the great secular religion of the late twentieth century, then there is no doubt that the Vitra Design Museum is going to become a pilgrimage chapel among devotees of the new faith.

As for the building's efficacy as a display space for the estimable collection of modern furniture assembled by Vitra International, it is too early to comment on its long-term success, but the variety of gallery configurations that Gehry has provided make it more than likely that a wide range of installations can be accommodated. These rooms include what Gehry has called the "plain Jane" galleries on the ground floor, and what is unquestionably the most exciting interior space Gehry has yet built: the upper gallery reached by either one of two curving staircases (expressed on the exterior) and illuminated by three separate skylights. Here Gehry uses light with all the confidence of a master well aware of how his architecture will work as a contained space, but also knowledgeable of how to make it seem almost infinite at the same time. The carefully considered deployment of the skylights, windows, and balcony looking down into the exhibition gallery on the ground floor below provide an ever-changing quality of light during the daytime, with artificial lighting available for specific illumination of the works on display. The informal arrangement of chairs on low platforms unencumbered by vitrines makes for more accessible viewing experience than is usually found in design museums, where objects are standardly displayed at an even greater physical remove from the visitor than old master paintings in an art gallery, an anomaly made all the more frustrating because objects of everyday use ought not to have the remoteness of archaeological rarities or religious relics.

In this spectacular upper gallery we see at last where Gehry's seemingly impetuous, but in fact quite methodical, experiments with architectural form have been leading him. This ultimate collision of the discrete forms that have been appearing in his designs over the last decade and a half has not resulted in the chaotic, "deconstructivist" space that so many of Gehry's critics have envisioned his work to represent, but rather an almost textbook definition of Le Corbusier's famous dictum on what architecture is:

"the skillful, correct, and magnificent play of volumes assembled in light." Here, in light conditions quite different from the flattening sunshine most typical of Los Angeles, Gehry shows himself beyond any further question to be an architect of international adaptability, an original creator of such sensitivity to the givens that every architect must take as his starting point that any initial unfamiliarity with the specifics of a place shrink to insignificance when gauged against his towering talent.

In his mischievous agglomeration of tilting towers, swirling staircases, flaring façades, and cantilevered canopies, Gehry provokes comparison with the architecture of German Expressionism – or that tiny proportion of it that was ever built. There have been Expressionist elements in Gehry's work at least since his unbuilt Wagner and Familian houses of 1978 for the Los Angeles-area communities of Malibu and Santa Monica respectively, though the particular contexts for those schemes seemed to imply an awareness of such local topographical phenomena as mudslides and earthquakes rather than the influence of Mendelsohn's Einstein Tower or "The Cabinet of Dr. Caligari." Nonetheless, Gehry's first executed design for Germany does indeed seem much more intentionally referential to the brief Expressionist tangent of German architecture between 1918 and 1923, after which a far more rational aesthetic (to say nothing of a parallel retrograde one) supplanted that moment during which intuition and a mystical belief in the power of crystalline forms caused a diversion from architecture's almost invariable historical adherence to the orthogonal rule.

That is about as close as Frank Gehry is likely to get to historical revivalism, and even at that he has gone about evoking a specific of architecture in his characteristically undogmatic manner. Gehry's is an "either/or" architecture, one which does not demand recognition of its antecedents, specific or general, in order to be understood under its own terms. Gehry's deliberate positioning of himself as an artist working in the medium of architecture is quite like that of Le Corbusier (even though Gehry does not pursue and demand recognition for simultaneous work in painting and sculpture as the Swiss-French master did). As Le Corbusier expressed it, "One uses stone, wood, cement, and turns them into

Wagner House, Malibu, California, 1978. Model.

Familian House, Santa Monica, California, 1978. Model.

Erich Mendelsohn. Einstein Tower, Potsdam, Germany, 1917–21.

houses or palaces; that's construction. It calls for skill. But suddenly, you touch my heart; you make me feel good. I am happy. I say: it's beautiful. This is architecture. It is art."

The Vitra Design Museum now takes its place among those museums that in the end become their own most precious artifact. Despite the small size of the Vitra building, it can without hyperbole be compared with Frank Lloyd Wright's Guggenheim Museum and Louis Kahn's Kimbell Museum as structures of such powerful architectural presence that they will always attract visitors for whom the buildings themselves, rather than the art or objects within them, is the major point of the journey. Like the Guggenheim and the Kimbell, the Vitra will also defy expansion, so complete and self-contained is the architects' vision of what the museum should be. None of those museums can be held up as a model for emulation in any way other than as a talisman of the audacity, imagination, and conviction that architecture at its greatest always embodies, no matter how various the means by which architects throughout the ages have achieved them. The Vitra Design Museum is a major landmark not just in Frank Gehry's increasingly impressive career, but in twentieth century architecture as a whole, evidence that on a contemporary scene clouded by imitation and regression, there is at least one master whose integrity of vision ensures that the century of modernism will not end without some of the hope with which it began.

Manufacturing the Sublime

Olivier Boissière

The factory is separated from the road by an orchard with trees in perfectly straight lines. From here you are first aware of the contrast between one building, obviously industrial, low and discreet, steely blue and metallic, elegant, blending with the landscape, austere and ostentatious at the same time, in the direct tradition of the engineer-architect and proud of it, and a second, a breaking wave of sharp and convoluted masses forming a united front, immediately astonishing because it is so respectful of the scale of its immediate neighbor and the surrounding countryside. If there is anything scandalous about this, it is the flagrant juxtaposition of two conflicting styles: the puritanical reserve of that kind of British architecture known as "high tech" and a proliferation of form which could not be called anything other than expressionist. One must also be aware that this grey and white configuration only works in the expansive framework of its general context, the area where the Rhine meets the Jura, with its own shapes and colors, its half-timbered houses of the kind once catalogued by Becher, its alternately dazzling and greyish light, its skies that are either low or infinite – and it only works in its intimate dialogue with a group of industrial buildings, the most recent of which shows a discreet and definitive sophistication. What we are looking at is the spectacle of two faces of contemporary architecture: the time difference between them (slight, scarcely a decade) will be reduced to nothing by history.

A sign of the times? symptom or consequence of the bankruptcy of ideologies? of the questioning of verities so far held to be universal? of the irresoluteness of the world and the end of the "great stories"? The architecture of the second half of the twentieth century is an unbroken parade of conflicts and theoretical struggles, the sign of a discipline in crisis. The "heroic" epoch of modern architecture maintained the debate at its most elementary level: a simple quarrel between the Ancients, champions of bourgeois and reactionary architecture, and the Moderns ("one must be absolutely modern" Rimbaud had said) for whom civic virtue, a sense of progress (and of history) and social utopia de facto made saints, at the same time heroes and martyrs, prophets and messiahs. After the Second World War the cause seemed to have been assimilated: the triumph of modern architecture was assured.

Until the late sixties the continuing presence of great masters like Frank Lloyd Wright, Mies van der Rohe, Le Corbusier or Álvar Aalto masked the fact that great principles and absolute truths had changed into dry and meaningless dogma. When they disappeared, an apparently homogeneous architectural milieu flew apart, and was put together again as a number of groups, tendencies, and schools, revolving around opposing poles a great distance apart: technology, sociology, a return to history, populism, or semiotics. One of Frank Gehry's strengths was that he assumed a singular destiny at an early stage. Attracted by the arts, educated at the University of Southern California in the modern architectural tradition, Frank Gehry steadily learned his trade in Pereira and Victor Gruen's great commercial agencies. Perhaps he could even have made a career with the latter if he had not decided to go his own way? Working with his fellow pupil Greg Walsh, young Frank Gehry's first buildings were influenced by others: perhaps by Raphael Soriano, the person who first made him want to be an architect, by Frank Lloyd Wright, a difficult influence to avoid, or by a certain Californian vernacular. He observed Louis Kahn and listened to Robert Venturi whilst keeping himself apart from what were supposed to be "great debates." Frank Gehry stuck to sound architectural principles: he was later to say, as if by whim: "I am the last functionalist!" But while the orphans of modernism were trying to recreate a theoretical and operational framework within the repertoire of historical, Renaissance and neo-classical archetypes and a (relative) autonomy of discipline, Frank Gehry, in his direct and instinctive fashion, was redicovering – if indeed it had been forgotten – that architecture is an art, a "technique" in the original Greek sense of the term, where material and spirit are reconciled.

The apple trees are in perfectly straight lines, and at this time of the year they have no leaves. Later, in spring, "flowers" will have "snowed down on to the branches," as the song has it. You will probably not want to sit down, but you can crouch in the lush, damp grass and contemplate the industrial site through the framework of the sculpture by Claes Oldenburg and Coosje van Bruggen, a slender construction of pincers, hammer and red and blue adjustable spanner, like an emblem of work or of the ingenuity of man. Behind it are the rolling hills, half-covered in a mist. Really the sculpture ought to be moved now that it has to relate to two blocks. But perhaps that isn't right, perhaps there ought to be another one. Plumper, swollen, exuberant, oozing sap. Who knows? But to the left we have metallic precision, tempered with perfect, rounded corners, and to the right an ancient bas-relief, alive with furious conflict.

A few paces into the avenue of trees in the meadow and you are on the axis of a street defined by Nicholas Grimshaw's steel-blue building and Frank Gehry's white box. At this point you will notice that the latter, in a friendly, neighborly gesture, has flown a sort of horizontal band between the two buildings – it is a covered footbridge. As you change your position it becomes clear that the façade, which seemed all of a piece, is on the move, and that it is in fact made up of elements placed in different planes: in the background is the front of the production unit, which will not be completely revealed until the museum is behind you; on the first plane – in the foreground – is the museum itself, leaning gently towards the west before its massive entrance awning appears all of a sudden; on the right – on the courtyard side – is the little gatehouse which dominates the entrance to the industrial site. At the moment all that can be seen of it is an oblique profile, rectangular in perspective, side by side with a trapezium with one side swollen into the arc of a circle. By moving a decent distance away – you will have to cross the road – it is possible to enjoy the ideal view: the eastern corner of the production unit, the north façade of the museum, the eastern corner of the unit, and the northern profile of the little gatehouse run precisely in an unbroken line. From then on you can come and go freely, move closer or further away, allow free play to the juxtapositions of shape, to the collisions of sharp bulk and circumvolution, to the changing view between the museum and the little gatehouse – everything the architect has been pleased to offer the curious observer. It's impossible to resist for long the temptation to climb to the level from which there is a panoramic view of the slightly sloping site, or that of walking to the picturesque little reservoir with its metal sphere perched on slender legs and its pointed hat, from which there is a view of the whole factory "in profile." It's easier then to understand Rolf Fehlbaum's intention of making the factory an urban group consisting of different shapes, either distinct or side by side: the original brick buildings, the little fifties building, touching in its ingenuity, with a base made up of little squares and an ashlar gable, the polyurethane canopy which makes it look bigger, swollen like a parachute, the wood and metal-mesh footbridge levitating above a meadow, the long building in ribbed board, then a pavilion in silky-soft concrete – an *agglomération* in a landscape which still speaks with a rural accent – *agglomération* is the indeterminate French word for any group of buildings, hamlet, village, town or city, and this trio made of white plaster and zinc, deep and glittering by turn, is the most recent addition to the category. If you go closer you will discover that this infinitely variable trinity is composed of – and decomposes into – parts, distinct amid identifiable items of bulk, as if endowed with a life all of its own: a strange process is at work here. Fragmentation as an architectural procedure appeared early in the work of Frank Gehry: in 1964 Lou Danziger's studio-residence – remarkably intact today in West Hollywood, on Melrose Avenue, otherwise changing all the time – is an example of two masses on a grid layout separated by a slender gap. Also, and this is only a decade later, in the Jung Institute project, 1976, where it is expressed in an open and explicit manner: within a closed precinct isolating the Institute from the outside world, half a dozen objects ("boxes") with varying geometry seem to float between the sky and a sheet of water reflecting them (the Jungian psyche…). From this project onwards fragmentation is to appear almost systematically in every project. Frank Gehry has provided diverse and convergent reasons for this. First of all, as a result of programmatic analysis, there is a will to clarify the project by isolating its constituent functional parts; then, in no particular order, comes a search for a precise scale, fascination with the "one-room-building… that has produced the most beautiful buildings in history," a taste for still life, for collage, a yearning for "sculpture." Thus each section is treated separately, endowed with its own form and identity by being played off in association or opposition against others, in order to recompose arrangements which are scattered or compact, softly detached or strictly ordered, always taking the surroundings, the constraints of

Studio-Residence for Lou Danziger, Hollywood, California, 1964. View from the rear.

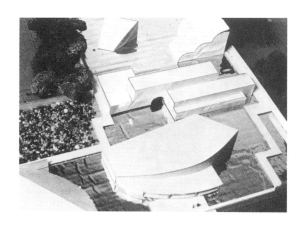

27

Jung Institute, Los Angeles, California, 1976. Model.

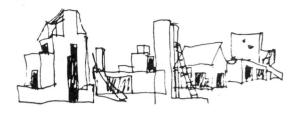

House for a Film Maker, Los Angeles, California, 1981. Sketch.

Gehry House, Santa Monica, California, 1978. Entrance side.

28

Frances Howard Goldwyn Regional Branch Library, North Hollywood, California, 1983–84. Model.

the programme and the intended function of the building into account, with minute care on the part of Frank Gehry for distances, intervals, and spaces in between. Different on-site re-composition strategies can be distinguished: free (house for a film maker, 1981; Loyola Law School, 1981–84); sunken (Gehry House, 1978; California Aerospace Museum, 1982–84); soundly assembled (Frances Howard Goldwyn Library, 1983–84); well-arranged (Benson house, 1981); fanned (Winton guest house, 1983); fanned and cruciform (Sirmai-Peterson house, 1984): as the years pass the process seems to move towards complexity and refinement, as if the architect were manipulating it with increasing mastery.

There is an innocent game you can play at Weil: trying to discover the elemental or "prime" (in the sense of a prime number) sections in the three buildings that make up Frank Gehry's contribution to the industrial complex, production, museum, and gatehouse; you would start with the most simple by detaching the parallel box from the trapezoid base with rounded façade, which are juxtaposed to form the gatehouse; you would then pass to the production unit and detach the north-eastern and north-western corners from the great placid box, splitting them down into curved ramps, aedicules and porches, finding the snakes and fish the architect has used; when you arrive at the museum you will notice first of all that its southern face is almost rectilinear. At one point in the project it could have been side by side with the production unit; then it was "drawn" north to the limit of the industrial precinct, a simple means of handling an off-site entrance for the public and a private entrance for administration and deliveries. Then you could remove the two placid south-facing boxes from the building, take off the three glazed masses capping the roofs and the out-of-true canopy marking the entrance, take away the square tower containing the elevator, detach the volute that contains the spiral staircase, then the slender bulk enclosing the second staircase, this one with a gentle curve. You would then be left with five main masses, five boxes, the first three making up entrance, foyer, and what is to be the conference room, the other two the tightly-knit exhibition galleries. Now you won't want to carry on playing the game of taking things apart: you will realize that you have at last come to the heart of the building, the kernel of the nut.

In the course of time Frank Gehry has forged an original language for himself. It is possible to assess the breadth of his development from his beginnings in the sixties down to his present work, which seems imbued with a sense of maturity, from the strict grid of the Danziger studio to the Vitra project's subtle profusion of tangled forms. It is possible to postulate three major poles: a surgical mode, already described (fragmentation followed by assembly), exploration of materials, appropriation of forms.

It is Frank Gehry's constant attention to art and artists that gave him his keen and unprejudiced eye for humble and unusual materials, often even despised in the architectural field. More than at any other time the artists of our century have intensified our sensitivity to urban landscape and conferred an unsuspected aesthetic charge upon the trivial. Collages and ready-mades were the signs which presaged this development, and pop art and the minimalists were its heralds. Frank Gehry's education came from contacts with the Johns, Rauschenberg, Judd, Andre, Serra, or the Californians around Larry Bell and Billy Al Bengston, Ed Moses and Ed Ruscha, all sensitive to urban and industrial reality and all of whom revelled in its truth and ruggedness. And Gehry transferred this sensibility to his architectural practice, with the eye of an aesthete and the fatal pragmatism of an architect. "Poor" materials were chosen for grain, texture, clean visual qualities then manipulated, twisted, tested in other contexts so that they were proven before being put to work in buildings. In the very early seventies Frank Gehry experimented with two materials which, although they were very different, had qualities in common, corrugated iron and corrugated cardboard. The use of iron produced two little buildings that marked a decisive step in the architect's work: the O'Neill hay barn, 1968, and the studio for artist Ron Davis, 1972. Gehry invented a range of furniture based on corrugated cardboard that was simple, supple, solid, and inexpensive: Easy Edges. Subsequently banal materials appear in Gehry's buildings in the Californian landscape, and the architect recycles them with the deliberate intention of conferring a different visual status upon them: examples are fence netting used to veil and cover fragments of his buildings; plywood left raw to respond to the stripped quality of his structures, all giving his work

Benson House, Los Angeles, California, 1981.

Sirmai-Peterson Residence, Thousand Oaks, California, 1984.

O'Neill Hay Barn, San Juan Capistrano, California, 1968.

Ron Davis House, Malibu, California, 1972.

"Easy Edges," range of furniture, 1969–73.

an aura of incompleteness (note incidentally that integrity of materials and structures was a leitmotiv of the purity of the moderns in their heroic period). Gradually Frank Gehry enriched his palette – his personal vocabulary – for the sake of his buildings: painted or galvanized iron, dark red Finnwood, zinc, copper, and lead are added to the ever-present plaster. Primary forms are also subjected to notable change: simple, well-behaved boxes on a grid are then distorted to provoke the intrusion of forced perspective. Then they swell imperceptibly to take on knife-blade profiles like those which, most perfectly expressed, haunt the work of Ellsworth Kelly. Gehry wants them to be even more fluid, more dynamic. From simple graffitti in the margins of notebooks, from seemingly unresolved jottings about the project (suspension points...), the figure of the fish has gradually imposed itself on Gehry almost naturally, almost in the way in which a question sometimes contains its own answer. It has inhabited his work in various forms. It has joined forces with the snake. At first it could have been passed off as a joke, an avatar of Venturi's "duck." Obviously it is no such thing. Today it asks the question which is never – or rarely – addressed: the question of the figure in architecture.

There is no historical precedent, no reference point to which to cling. Figures, human or animal, never occur other then as emblematic signs on the fringes of the discipline: the Colossus of Rhodes or the enigmatic enigma of the Sphinx; you might find grimacing Atlases or impassive caryatids under palace balconies, or heroes on acroteria and dolphins in capricious friezes. In its monumental version, free or applied, figures are usually derived from statuary. It would certainly be convenient to deal with Frank Gehry's fish and other accompanying figures by calling them "sculptures," but then they would always have to be accorded this status. In the Kobé Fish-Dance restaurant, 1987, for example, the standing fish can be taken as a monumental sign (in this sense it is to some extent a "duck" in the manner of Venturi). But what can one say about a coiled snake that "is" a building? Another way of evading the question would be to identify Gehry's creatures as pure symbols. Frank Gehry himself has explained the appearance of fish as a derisive reply to post-modernists who draw upon Renaissance or neo-classical architecture: if one has to look for sources in the past, why not go even further back, into pre-history and the very origins of the world and of men? People have also not failed to invoke the symbolism of which the fish is bearer, for Gehry personally as a memory of infancy and fetish of the Jewish culinary tradition, or as a sign of re-cognition for early Christians, an astrological sign, even a sexual sign (in this context one must point to certain drawings by Gehry where the head of the fish is explicitly in the form of a pe-nis, and thus unambiguous). But it does not seem that Gehry uses it as such, even if he is fully aware of the rich symbolic charge that it con-veys. No. The fish is used for what it is: a reser-voir of extended and compact forms, of texture and iridescent colors which Gehry freely incor-porates into his architectural vocabulary in a spirit which doubtless brings him close to cer-tain expressionists in this century, Scharoun or Gaudí. With his figures, the fish, the snake, the trees (at Rebecca's and Main Street Building for Chiat/Day, 1988), Gehry has tackled primitive naturalism at a point where suspicion of the sacred seems to be dawning.

You could smile for a moment about the incon-gruous idea that the serpentine coils of Vitra writhe two paces away from a row of apple trees. You will smile again on passing under the massive awning suspended above the entrance to the museum, through a door which is daringly out of true. You then come to the foyer: you will stop dead as you realize that from this precise point you can take in all the space enclosed within the exterior of the building: on the left, the cafeteria, on the right the clear space in-tended for a conference room; in front of one is the first, high gallery, then further away, through an opening preceded by a few staggered steps, a second, and then up there, the third, suggested across the almost pyramidic space half-masking the point at which the cruciform window springs. You will notice, not without a little sur-prise, that the building's orgy of colliding form is transmuted into serenity once you are inside. You stroll around clean, calm, white space. No openings to the outside world to disturb the in-triguing spectacle of the collection amassed by Rolf Fehlbaum, a collection of chairs, armchairs, stools and seats of all kinds covering industrial production from the beginning of the nineteenth century to the present day, said to contain about

Fish lamp, 1983.

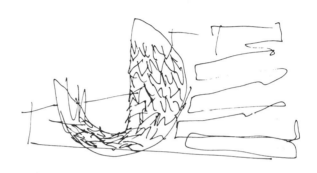

Fish-Dance Restaurant, Kobé, Japan, 1987.

twelve hundred items. You will first of all be surprised that this apparently sensible man should be devoted to this repertoire with a passion which psychologists say is based in regression, compensation, and even exorcism of death. You will rapidly understand what, for one of the great industrialists in the field, an accumulation of experiments of this kind can represent. What if this morbid hunger, futile at first sight, concealed a crazy ambition for total knowledge in a quest that was almost initiatory? Then you will observe each model with a new eye, trying to imagine the sum of risks and adventures of which it was the object. You will know that each one represents the concretization of a piece of knowledge at a given moment in the advancement of technology, an attempt which was always being started over again to reach perfection in the expression of a form, an exemplary moment in the ingeniousness of the human spirit. One will also better understand the complicity which links the collecting industrialist and his architect.

Frank Gehry shows great faith in man, in his capacity unfailingly to invent, in his inextinguishable desire for new discoveries. This belief, both instinctive and reflective, is accompanied in the architect by a constant taste for work, for making things by hand, for "craft." This may seem paradoxical: after all, Gehry made his name with work for which he himself claimed an element of the incomplete. A better explanation came later: Gehry, according to one of his Californian fellow-architects, is an "architect of crisis." He manages starvation budgets successfully, and is clear-minded enough to make out their limits; he knows how to draw a personal aesthetic from them in the spirit of the artists he was observing. In his work in the seventies he made, as they say, a virtue of necessity; his results derive, in a certain sense, from poor art. This was also suited to a particular period, a moment in which a changing society was exalting the values of the ephemeral, of mobility and of impermanence. The lightness of Gehry's buildings, their adaptability, their ease in admitting modifications or additions are in tune with the spirit of the times. Gehry has improved the quality of his buildings while remaining faithful to "honest" handling of detail and finishing touches by making them participate in the construction process itself, without recourse to application or camouflage.

What is one to say about the thinking of the architect when it is expressed only in scant signs that have to be hunted down at the point where an intention changes direction, or in the everyday world of his work? Michael Heizer said something one day, on the occasion of a visit to Complex One, the artist's mastaba in the Nevada desert, which suggested that Gehry should build more durably (William Burroughs said that posterity depends only on itself). There are evocative drawings of pueblos belonging to the ancestral culture of the Southwest. There are repeated allusions to Tournus and Autun, and his admiration for Romanesque architecture constantly shows through. Materials get heavier and heavier, dense, timeless, almost alchemic, zinc, copper, lead. To say nothing about fish and snakes from the mists of time. These traces seem to show decisive yet unacknowledged direction in this man who is eloquent and modest, open and secretive. They bear witness, perhaps, to a sense of new gravity, the conscience of the times, a mad and modest will to write one's name there (and thus to escape from it).

You walk through the galleries one by one. Like every visitor, without a single exception, at the precise moment at which you pass through the opening leading to the lower gallery you will stop, as if struck by an invisible force, and raise your eyes to the great cruciform expanse of stained glass with its clouds running in the sky. Without knowing why, you will spare a thought for Malevich. You will make use of a medieval spiral staircase. Then you will be in what the artist called his "crypt," a great white space with a vault with cruciform beams. And there you will remain, seized by the magic of a place that has been stripped, a monastic place, with its meagre components – a wooden floor, a few bases and their objects – lit, one ought to say "illuminated" or "dazzled," by an indescribable light. It comes from above, soft, lively, almost palpable. You will remain for a long time to contemplate introspectively the tender halo lavishly produced by a deep niche and the pointed splash of light from a tall triangular crack; it will not cross your mind to wonder why other visitors are whispering as if intimidated. Later, sitting in the foyer, you will collect your thoughts. You will amuse yourself with the idea that this museum is designed like a church with nave, choir, crypt, and ambulatory, and if you have a facetious eye, even a sacristy

Le Corbusier. "Staggered pyramid" at Ronchamp chapel.

and presbytery. The architect has built a shelter for the patron-industrialist's collection that is at the same time joyous and dignified, a sort of mausoleum that perhaps Hans Magnus Enzensberger would not disown. Who knows? You will go out again, and walk in the wet grass. The plaster enfolding the lively shapes will have gained depth with the declining day. Later it will paint its face with the gilded dust of the setting sun. And there we have it: art. That emotion where joyous exaltation and a hint of anguish mix. A sense of vertigo when confronted with mystery. The officiating priest, a grotesque clown, a daring young man on a flying trapeze, a climber of Everest, an artist, suddenly appeared at the turning-point of life to redeem its pettiness. He takes risks, he puts himself in danger. Gehry will stay in the memory for a long time, under his great black umbrella, perched on the little staggered pyramid at the edge of the valley, contemplating Le Corbusier's Ronchamp chapel with the wondering look of a child. Above the altar is a great boat thrown off balance, like Noah's Ark stranded on the mountain-side. One day, Gehry took up the torch. Armed with his pencils, his crumpled paper, his models in pinned card, with concrete, iron, and breeze blocks, girded about with powerful or pitiful instruments, surrounded by his companions, humble or grand, Gehry tried to manufacture the sublime.

Construction of Vitra Design Museum and Furniture Production Unit

Building owner:
Vitra Verwaltungs GmbH, 7858 Weil am Rhein

Design:
Frank O. Gehry & Associates
Santa Monica, California/USA

Responsible for the design:
Frank O. Gehry, FAIA

Project Manager:
Robert G. Hale, AIA

Design Project, supervision:
C. Gregory Walsh, AIA

Project Architect:
Berthold H. Penkhues

Project Assistants:
C. J. Bonura
Edwin Chan

Planning and supervision of construction:
Architekten GPF + Assoziierte
Günter Pfeifer
Roland Mayer
Lörrach

Project Direction:
Roland Mayer

Assistants:
Susanne Schlönvogt
Sabine Holzmann
Kristina Trcovic
Bernhard Flüge
Jacek Dominiak
Rafael Novoa

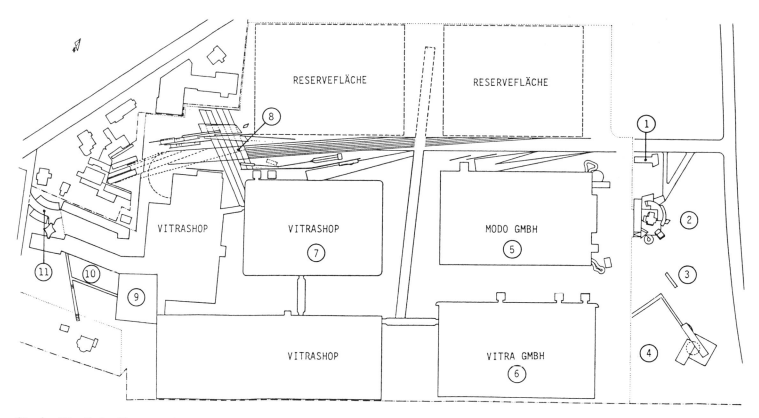

Site plan, Vitra Design Museum and
industrial buildings of the
Vitra Gesellschaften.

Key:
1   Gatehouse. Arch. F. O. Gehry & Ass.
    and GPF + Ass. – Günter Pfeifer,
    Roland Mayer
2   Vitra Design Museum.
    Arch. F. O. Gehry & Ass. and
    GPF + Ass.
3   Sculpture »Balancing Tools« by
    Claes Oldenburg and
    Coosje van Bruggen
4   Pavilion. Arch. Tadao Ando & Ass.
    and GPF + Ass.
5   Furniture production unit.
    Arch. F. O. Gehry & Ass. and
    GPF + Ass.
6–7 Furniture production unit.
    Arch. Nicholas Grimshaw & Partners
8   Fire house. Arch. Zaha M. Hadid
    and GPF + Ass.
9   Showroom. Arch. Antonio Citterio
10 Walkway. Arch. Antonio Citterio
11 Parking and entrance.
    Arch. Eva Jiricna

38–39
View of the museum from the north-
eastern production unit access ramp.
Bicycle shed on the right.

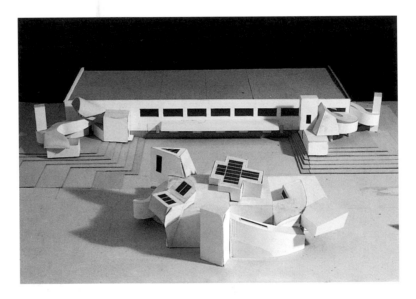

Model of museum (below) and production
unit (above) with side access ramps.

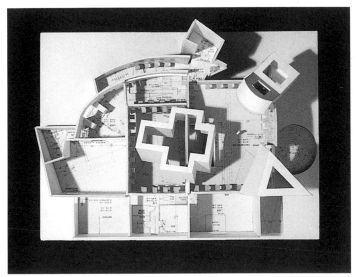

Bird's-eye views of museum model with
roof removed.

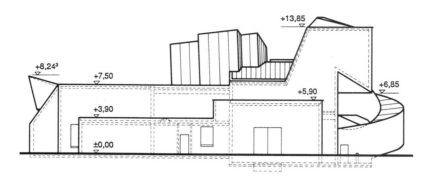

+13,85

+8,24³ +7,50 +5,90 +6,85

+3,90

±0,00

Elevation of museum from the south-west.
Scale 1:400.

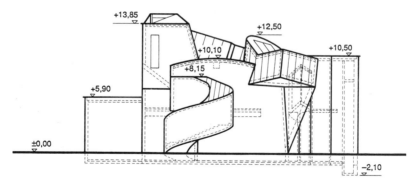

+13,85 +12,50

+10,10 +10,50

+8,15

+5,90

±0,00

−2,10

Elevation from the south-east.

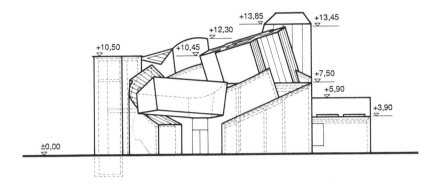

Elevation from the north-east.

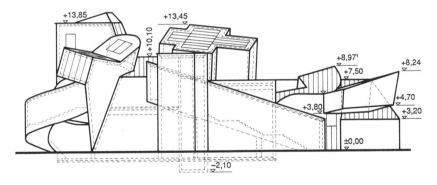

Elevation from the north-west.

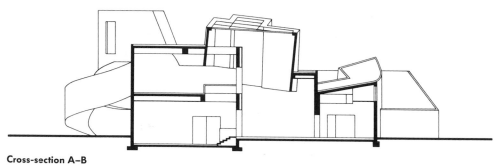

Cross-section A–B

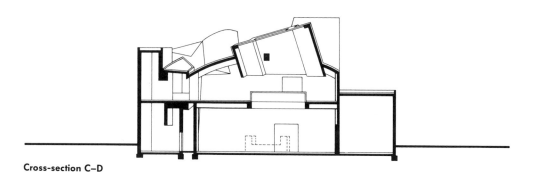

Cross-section C–D

Cross-section E–F

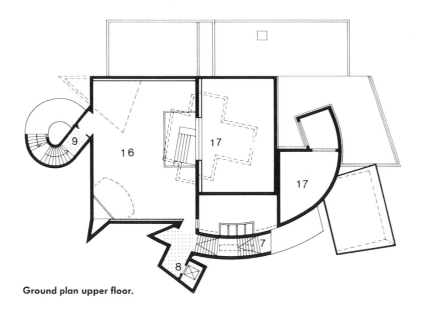

Ground plan upper floor.

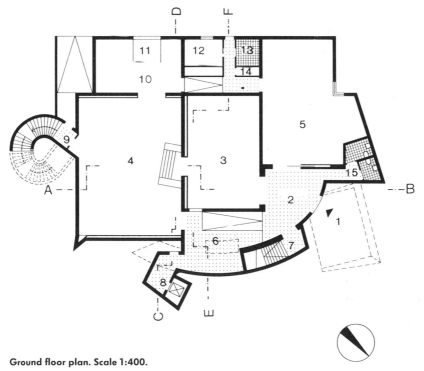

Ground floor plan. Scale 1:400.

Key: 1 entrance; 2 foyer; 3 two-story
central exhibition space; 4 large exhibition
space; 5 exhibition/conference room;
6 cafeteria; 7 access to upper story;
8 elevator; 9 spiral staircase to upper
story; 10 storeroom; 11 hydraulic ramp;
12 office; 13 kitchen; 14 service facilities;
15 bathroom; 16 upper story exhibition
space; 17 airspace.

46–47
Upper story exhibition space with
"masterpieces" of 19th and 20th century
chair design.

View of Weil from the Tüllinger Höhe
looking towards the Rhine valley. In the
middle ground is the Vitra factory site, in
front of it the access road to the industrial
estate Weil.

View of the entire complex. On the right is
the museum with gatehouse in front of the
new production unit, on the left and
behind the Gehry buildings, Nicholas
Grimshaw's factory buildings. Gehry's
three buildings, uniformly executed in
white plaster and grey titanium zinc
sheeting, stand out from the other factory
buildings.

View through the vines of museum and
new production unit.

54

View of museum from road. In the background on the left is a factory building by
Nicholas Grimshaw, on the right the access ramp to canteen and large showroom
in the new production unit. The gatehouse
is on the extreme right.

52–53
Museum in front of production unit north
façade. The façade with ramps worked out
down to the last three-dimensional detail
provides a visual background making
a formal connection with the museum.

Entrance to the museum with its projecting
canopy. Museum and production unit
access ramp make up a formal unit.

The furniture production unit (left in the picture) with lateral edges emphasized by towers. In the short end of the building opposite the museum are the ground floor production section and loading ramp and upper story with dispatch department. Showroom of Vitra furniture and canteen are reached by side ramps.

The sculpture "Balancing Tools" by Claes
Oldenburg and Coosje van Bruggen.

Road between museum with gatehouse
and production unit.

The group of buildings from the opposite
direction with view towards Weil.

Interplay of shapes of production unit and
museum.

Nicholas Grimshaw's factory buildings in bluish-grey high tech architecture with metal façades (in the background on the left) makes an impressive composition in combination with Frank Gehry's buildings.

The north side of the museum with main entrance.

The soaring canopy is a powerful accent
in the restrained entrance area. The
canopy is open, revealing its daring
construction. The high window is made
rectangular in contrast with the curved
shape of the ramp.

Roofs of the east side of production unit
and museum. White plastered walls form
a contrast with roofs and wall sections
clad in titanium zinc.

Exterior design was the result of intensive discussion between Frank Gehry and Günter Pfeifer, the executive architect in Lörrach. Originally the outer cladding was to be in sheet steel, "like an old oil-can," said Gehry. The white plastered surfaces are the result of an intensive intercontinental fax discussion, and "there is sheet steel wherever it gets rained on," said the German half of the conversation.

The sculptural directness of the exterior
offers the viewer an enormous range of
experience in the lavishness of its detail.

Museum service tract on the factory road.
On the right the storeroom with hydraulic
ramp, the small entrance on the left leads
to office and service rooms. The volumes
of this side are designed in such a way
as to correspond with the opposite façade
of the production unit.

In contrast with this, all the other sides are developed as continuous architectural sculpture, constantly changing in their articulation through contrasts in light and materials.

A rectangular volume is placed in front of
the exhibition rooms. The large door leads
into the storeroom for exhibits.

Crystalline and organic building shapes
continually form contrasts further
enhanced by light.

The powerful curves in the gently inclined access ramps (right-hand side here) to the first floor of the production unit are not only formally justified but contribute to extend the climb in a pleasant fashion.

By the wall of American furniture in the
central exhibition space is a view through
to the cafeteria.

78–79
View from the foyer of the central two-
story exhibition space. On the left is the
cafeteria, in the background the large
exhibition space, five steps lower. In the
right-hand foreground the chair "Dan
Darre" by John Mills.

The view into the central exhibition space
shows an impressive interplay of light
falling from many different directions.
In the corner is "Little Beaver" by
Frank Gehry.

In the central exhibition space two sets of scaffolding show a juxtaposition of seating from the USA (left) and Europe (right) from the start of industrial production in the 19th century till today.

In the right-hand foreground is the "Well-Tempered Chair," an armchair in sprung sheet steel by Ron Arad.

86

From the central exhibition space in the
background, five steps lead down the
large exhibition space. The floor of the
ground floor is in non-reflective painted
composition flooring.

This room is also lit from a section of the
cruciform glass roof.

"Floating shapes" – an exhibition with
pioneering models by Charles Eames and
international bentwood designs on the
plinths – an example of a typical Vitra
Design Museum presentation.

The opening in the wall provides a pic-
ture-like view of the display of European
chair designs – from Thonet to Arne
Jacobsen.

The cafeteria area, slightly separated,
gives a view of the large exhibition space.

From the foyer – the cash-desk counter is
in the foreground – there is access to the
exhibition/conference room, here showing
the "Friends Exhibition" (see also page 95).
Here again we see interplay of vertical
and horizontal openings, formed contra-
puntally of spatial and light volumes.

Steps from the foyer to the upper story.
The rectangular high window (see page 63)
provides light for the stairway and a
formal contrast with the curve of the ramp.

97
The large exhibition space in the upper
story with classics of furniture design:
chairs by Thonet, Hoffmann, Rietveld, Mies
van der Rohe, Breuer, Panton.

98

The clarity of the rectangular ground plan
is overcome by the expressive forms of the
wall and ceiling openings. The direct and
indirect sources of light thus created give
the room a magic quality.

The upper exhibition space gives an
unrestricted view into the two rooms
below.

The cross of light which is an integral part
of the interplay of forms concludes this
building made up of space and light.

Photography credit

The photographs on pages 11–31 and 40–41
were made available by Frank Gehry.
Richard Bryant took the photos of the
Vitra Design Museum on pages 38–39 and
49–101.
Lucien Hervé took those on pages 19 and 34.
Robert Winkler took the lower photo on
page 18.
The plans on pages 42–45 are reprinted with
the kind permission of *DBZ – Deutsche Bau-
zeitschrift.*